OSPREY
PUBLISHING

Siege Weapons of the Far East (1)

AD 612–1300

Stephen Turnbull · Illustrated by Wayne Reynolds

First published in Great Britain in 2001 by Osprey Publishing,
Elms Court, Chapel Way, Botley, Oxford OX2 9LP, United Kingdom.
Email: info@ospreypublishing.com

ISBN 1 84176 339 X

Editor: Simone Drinkwater
Design: Melissa Orrom Swan
Index by Alan Rutter
Originated by Grasmere Digital Imaging, Leeds, UK
Printed in China through World Print Ltd.

01 02 03 04 05   10 9 8 7 6 5 4 3 2 1

FOR A CATALOGUE OF ALL BOOKS PUBLISHED BY OSPREY MILITARY
AND AVIATION PLEASE CONTACT:

The Marketing Manager, Osprey Direct UK, PO Box 140,
Wellingborough, Northants, NN8 4ZA, United Kingdom.
Email: info@ospreydirect.co.uk

The Marketing Manager, Osprey Direct USA,
c/o Motorbooks International, PO Box 1,
Osceola, WI 54020-0001, USA.
Email: info@ospreydirectusa.com

www.ospreypublishing.com

Dedication

To my brother, Andrew Turnbull

Artist's Note

Readers may care to note that the original paintings from which the colour
plates in this book were prepared are available for private sale. All reproduction
copyright whatsoever is retained by the Publishers. All enquiries should be
addressed to:

Wayne Reynolds, 20 Woodside Place, Burley, Leeds LS4 2QU UK

The Publishers regret that they can enter into no correspondence upon this
matter.

SIEGE WEAPONS OF THE FAR EAST (1) AD 612–1300

INTRODUCTION

These books are concerned with the machinery of siegecraft as used by Chinese, Korean, Mongol and Japanese armies between about 612, when the Sui dynasty invaded Korea, and 1644, when Beijing fell to the Manchus, although the title could easily have been 'Ancient and Medieval Chinese Siege Weapons' with a time span ranging back as far as 500 BC. No country has such a long and distinguished military history as China, and almost all of the devices described in the pages that follow originated from ancient China.

Yet all siege weapons must be understood in the context for which they were created, which was to attack or defend a fortified place, and it is for this reason that the study of how these machines were used by China's neighbours is most rewarding. Each country provided its own context into which the siege weapons were fitted, and certain distinctive differences between them reveal both strengths and weaknesses in the machines themselves, also raising questions about cultural attitudes to siegecraft and even to the practice of war itself. During the period covered by these books, therefore, all the above military cultures interacted with each other in turn, borrowing, copying, imitating and sometimes discarding Chinese siege weapons according to their appropriateness for the local terrain, social situation or military tradition. The common link is the use of the weaponry described here, which was adopted, adapted and improved over a very long period of time. This accounts for the overlap in time periods between the two volumes, which have been designed around weapon types, and divided to give two books of equal size.

As these books are concerned with machines rather than events, the particular historical examples chosen to illustrate their use in words and pictures, have been selected because they show the particular weapon's operation in the clearest way. Of the 14 colour plates in the two volumes, no less than ten have a background of sieges conducted during the time of the Song dynasty, the golden age of siege weaponry in China. Yet the historical continuity is quite amazing, because even the key introduction of gunpowder in about 950 did not bring about the

Stringing a hand-held crossbow, showing the composite nature of the bow's construction. This infantry weapon was used in sieges for many centuries. (Japan Archive)

demise of the siege weapons of ancient times. Instead, these tried and trusted machines continued to be used alongside and in conjunction with cannon until the very end of our period. For example, during the siege by the Chinese of the Japanese fort of Sach'on, in Korea during 1598, we find a modern cannon being mounted on to a wheeled battering ram of a design identical to models used more than 1000 years earlier.

Research for these books has involved a huge amount of difficult work, and my search of the literature has revealed that there is no surer way to destroy one's academic reputation than to attempt to reconstruct siege weapons! Many organisations and individuals have assisted me in trying to overcome this. I list their names below, but take full responsibility for what follows. I would like to acknowledge in particular the help and suggestions received from Dr David Nicolle; Ian Bottomley; Thom Richardson; William Lindesay of 'Wild Wall Walks', Beijing; the library staff of the Royal Armouries, Leeds; the War Memorial, Seoul; Osaka Castle Museum and the Museum of Chinese History, Beijing. I thank most of all my wife, who always makes the most sensible suggestions.

SIEGE WARFARE IN THE FAR EAST AD 612–1300

China

The particular context of Chinese siegecraft was the fortified town, which was where the wealth of ancient China was located. These towns and cities were a lure and a target for rebels and raiders alike over many centuries. Chinese dynasties thus came and went to the accompaniment of much siege warfare, and early versions of siege crossbows and traction trebuchets may be noted in the accounts of the wars of the Qin and Han dynasties, and appear in the early military writings associated with the name of Mo Zi. Centuries later, trebuchets were used in the conquest of the Sui by the Tang in 617, and later during the fall of the Tang and the wars between the Song and the Khitan Liao dynasties.

The design and use of siege weapons reached a peak under the Northern and Southern Song dynasties (960–1279), and their names will appear in connection with many of the weapons described in the pages that follow. The Song nonetheless suffered a severe setback early in the twelfth century. In northern Manchuria, beyond the territory held by the Liao, tribes known as the Jurchen had risen to power. They

The fortified town or city provided the context for Chinese siege warfare. This drawing reconstructs a typical wide rampart, narrow entrance and ditch defence system that would be found up until the time of the Tang and Song dynasties. (Japan Archive)

East gate of Zhenbiancheng, a rare example of a fortified village near to, but not on, the Great Wall in Hebei Province. (Photograph by William Lindesay)

rebelled against the Liao in 1114 and the next year adopted the dynastic name of Jin. The Song, hoping to regain territories lost to the Liao, unwisely allied themselves to the Jin and helped in the destruction of the Liao, which was achieved in 1125. However, when the Song showed themselves to be dissatisfied with their share of the spoils, the Jin continued their aggressive moves towards the south, and in 1126 captured Kaifeng, the Song capital.

From this time on, Song hegemony was limited to southern China, so that the dynasty then became known as Southern Song. For a while they continued to fight back against the Jin, and conducted operations from their new capital of Hang-zhou from 1135 onwards. In 1153, the Jin moved their capital to the site of present-day Beijing. As we will see in the sections which follow, much use was made of the best siege technology by both sides, as the Southern Song attempted to regain their territories in northern China over the next 50 years, while the Jin mounted a fierce counter-offensive against them. The Southern Song city of De'an in Hubei successfully withstood no less than eight siege attempts between 1127 and 1132, and bitter hostilities continued until both dynasties had to face the dramatic new threat posed by the Mongols.

Korea

After many centuries of peace, which arose from being left alone while internal strife continued in China, Korea was invaded by a Chinese army in 612. At the time, Korea was divided into the three kingdoms of Koguryo, Silla and Paekche. The attack was led by an emperor of the Sui dynasty, who unsuccessfully attacked the northernmost Korean state of Koguryo. Their failure led to the Sui dynasty being replaced by the Tang, who themselves moved against Koguryo in 645. The Tang army did not press on as far as the Sui had done, and at first contented itself with attacking Koguryo possessions in Liaodong. The fortified town of Liaodong was

A portcullis that could be lowered over a Chinese gateway in the event of the gate being destroyed. (Japan Archive)

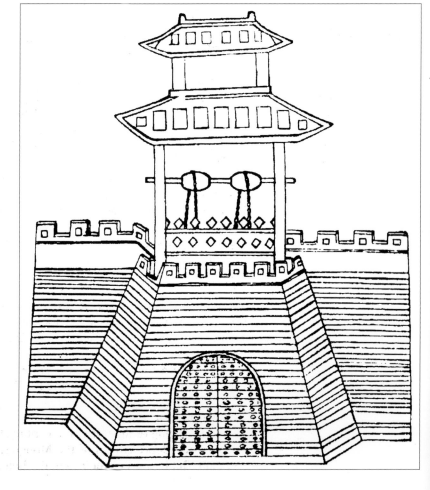

besieged, and succumbed when a tower was set alight and a strong wind fanned the flames, engulfing the whole town. Nearby Ansi was not to be captured so easily, holding out for a further 60 days until winter began. Korean winters are particularly severe, as the freezing winds blow straight down from Siberia, making both the temperature and the terrain unpleasant and unsuitable for campaigning. As a result of the defenders' persistence, the Tang army withdrew to suffer a long and miserable retreat home, and Ansi was saved.

In 666, the Tang invaded once again and laid siege to the Koguryo capital of P'yongyang. The city fell after a month-long siege and 20,000 prisoners were taken. The Tang were eager to make the whole of Korea their vassal state, and wars between Tang and Silla began. When neither side

The gateway of a Korean city, shown here in its reconstructed form, on the island of Kanghwa, north-east of Seoul. (Japan Archive)

gained the upper hand, negotiations were held, which allowed Silla to control almost the whole of the Korean peninsula while the Tang retained the Koguryo territory in Manchuria. This was the beginning of Korea's golden age, which saw the development of Buddhism and a flowering of science and culture centred around the Silla capital of Kyongju.

The glorious Silla state lasted only a century, and in 935 the Koryo dynasty was founded by King T'aejo. However, a new threat was developing to the north, because the Khitan tribes, who originated in Mongolia, had taken over the Liaodong area and founded the Liao dynasty. The Khitans raided Korea over the next century, and even captured Kaesong, the Koryo's capital, in 1011. The Koreans resisted the Khitans from walled towns on the Chinese model and also from numerous sansongs (mountain fortresses). These were characterised by a style of castle building that used small, flat stones to build walls that snaked up and down the contours of the land, with little contouring of the slope by excavation except for the sites of gates or towers. Both varieties of Korean fortification had already seen the employment of Chinese siege weapons in the wars against the Sui and the Tang, and there was soon to be much more siege activity in response to the new arrivals on the military scene of the Far East: the Mongols.

The Mongols

At the beginning of the thirteenth century, both China and Korea began to suffer the depredations of the Mongols, who preferred to deal with the main field forces of their enemies before advancing far into hostile

territory where there were likely to be fortified places. As Chinggis Khan's unsuccessful siege of the Xixia capital in 1209 illustrated, the Mongols' whirlwind mounted operations tended to come to a halt at a well-defended town wall, but by using the military ability for which they were to become renowned, these fierce horsemen rapidly acquired the techniques of siegecraft. These included making extensive use of captives skilled in siege technology, where such men were to become an important channel for the dissemination of Chinese siegecraft throughout much of the known world.

The Mongol advance against the Jin empire began in 1211, and much of the effort was directed towards capturing Zhongdu (modern Beijing). In 1214, the Jin emperor decided to move the imperial residence to the old Song capital of Kaifeng, which was protected to the north by the Yellow River. The Mongols saw this as a provocation, so the siege of Beijing was pressed forward with even greater vigour, and when it fell in May 1215 it was systematically sacked and partially destroyed by fire. In 1227, Chinggis Khan died, which gave the Jin some respite from Mongol attacks until Ogedei Khan resumed operations by sending his famous general Subadai against Kaifeng in 1231. The Jin defended themselves by using iron-cased bombs and fire lances, but the city fell the following year, and the Jin empire finally surrendered in 1234.

The Mongols had also fought alongside the Koreans against the Khitans in 1218, where their success led them to demand an enormous tribute from the Koryo rulers. When this was opposed, a Mongol invasion of Korea took place in 1231. The Mongol general Sartaq

Details of the simple wall of a Korean sansong (mountain castle) at Chukju, the site of a fierce siege by the Mongols in 1235. The walls are built from small stones and snake up and down the slopes of the mountain, with no attempt being made to level the contours by excavation. (Japan Archive)

A wide and flat crossbow platform on a city wall of the Song dynasty. This was almost certainly intended to provide a location for siege crossbows as well as hand-held ones. (Japan Archive)

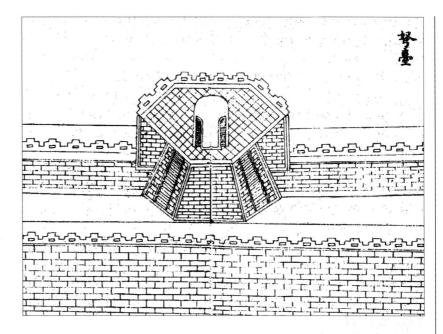

crossed the Yalu and headed south to begin a long siege of the city of Kuju. Even though Mongol catapults breached the walls in 200 places, Kuju held out. When a separate Mongol army headed south to threaten Kaesong, the Koryo government moved to the island of Kanghwa. The Mongols were no sailors, and Kanghwa held out against all Mongol attempts at assault, even though the distance from the mainland to the island at its nearest point was only half a mile.

In August 1232, General Sartaq invaded Korea again, and ravaged the places that the Korean king had abandoned. He then laid siege to a small sansong called Ch'oin, which was defended by a redoubtable warrior-monk named Kim Yun-hu. Kim was a skilled archer and, as the Mongol horde approached, he succeeded in putting an arrow into Sartaq's eye. With their commander dead, the Mongols withdrew, only to return in 1235 and pillage Korea until the government in exile on Kanghwa island was forced to surrender as the rest of Korea was burned around them.

Having defeated the Xixia, the Jin and the Koreans, the Mongols pressed forward their conquest of the Southern Song from 1254 onwards in a huge operation hindered temporarily by the death of Mongke Khan in 1259. The effort was resumed by Khubilai Khan, with a major battle at Diaoyu in Sichuan province in 1265, and the campaign which followed proved to be a colossal military undertaking that faced numerous obstacles. The Mongol armies were not used to the climate or the terrain of the south, and also faced formidable walled towns such as Xiangyang on the Han River, which was besieged between 1268 and 1274. However, the extent of the Mongol conquests allowed them to bring new siege weapons to China, of which the most important was the Muslim counterweight trebuchet, first used at Xiangyang in 1272. From Xiangyang onwards, Mongol siege artillery played an increasingly decisive role in the war against the Southern Song. One by one, their town walls crumbled under the battering from trebuchets, and the last Song supporters finally capitulated in 1279. This led to the establishment

The tower of a Japanese yamashiro, from a painted screen in the Watanabe Museum, Tottori. A samurai is climbing up using a simple scaling ladder. The context of Japanese siege warfare was totally different from continental Asia, with an almost complete absence of fortified towns. (Japan Archive)

of the Mongol Yuan dynasty of China and from the beginning of the fourteenth century the terms 'Mongol' and 'Chinese' siege warfare are synonymous.

Meanwhile, in 1273, a daughter of Khubilai Khan had been married to a Korean crown prince, so that the two countries were officially united. Control of Korea allowed Khubilai Khan to use its resources and its geographical position for his most ambitious enterprise of all – the invasion of Japan. The first landing, in 1274, was driven off by Japanese bravery in spite of the Mongols' use of exploding bombs. A second invasion, in 1281, was carried out on a much greater scale, appearing likely to succeed in establishing a permanent bridgehead, when the Mongol fleet, lying at anchor to avoid Japanese raiding parties, was suddenly hit by a typhoon, the famous kamikaze. The survivors retired to

Korea, and the invasion was over. Khubilai Khan also mounted campaigns against Vietnam, Burma and Java. Although several accounts mention the Mongols attacking fortified places, apart from a reference to using exploding bombs as a signalling device in Java, there are no details available of the siege weapons they took with them.

Japan

For almost all of the period discussed above, Japan was engaged in wars of its own in which siege warfare often played an important role, and from about AD 400, Japanese armies were involved in wars in Korea in support of the Paekche state. This activity reached its peak during the seventh century, when Japan sent expeditionary forces to aid Paekche against the alliance of Silla and Tang China. This adventure came to an end with a disastrous defeat at the Paekch'on River in 663, and from 666, when the Tang defeated Koguryo, Japan moved on to the defensive in the face of a likely invasion by Silla.

The walls of a Japanese yamashiro, from a painted screen in the Watanabe Museum, Tottori, showing the almost total reliance the Japanese placed on wood as a building material prior to the sixteenth century. (Japan Archive)

Much military lore passed into Japan at this time, and Japanese armies of the eighth century used large siege crossbows against rebel fortresses. However, as these were never the primary weapons of the Japanese army, they were finally abandoned in about 1200.

Japan was largely isolated and comparatively peaceful during the thirteenth century. This meant that any advances in siege warfare associated with the spread of the Mongol Empire, such as the counter-weight trebuchet, largely passed it by. Even the shock delivered by the Mongol invaders in 1274 and their use of exploding bombs had a surprisingly limited influence on Japan, where there was already a very different tradition and context of siege warfare. Unlike the walled towns of China and Korea, fortified places in Japan tended to be isolated military outposts. These yamashiro (mountain castles) were hilltop fortresses consisting only of wooden stockades, gates and towers, joined to one another across valleys and peaks to form a complex defensive arrangement. With no stone or mudbrick walls to batter down, these castles were almost always overcome by infantry assault, often supported by arson attacks launched by fire arrows. Throughout Japanese history, large-scale missile weapons such as siege crossbows appear to have been used mainly as anti-personnel devices.

CROSSBOW SIEGE ARTILLERY

Non-gunpowder siege artillery may be classified according to the source of the energy imparted to the projectile, which may be provided by the tension in the shaft of a bow, as in the large-scale crossbow, or by the tension in twisted sinew, although this latter form of propulsion does not appear to have been used at all in the Far East. Alternatively, the energy may be provided through rotary motion around a pivot, either from men pulling on ropes (the traction trebuchet) or from the force of a descending weight (the counterweight trebuchet).

The Chinese siege crossbow

In its hand-held version, the crossbow was the standard weapon of the early Chinese armies, originating around the fourth century BC and reaching its level of perfection within three centuries. The bronze

A multiple-bolt, single-bow siege crossbow mounted on a static frame. (Japan Archive)

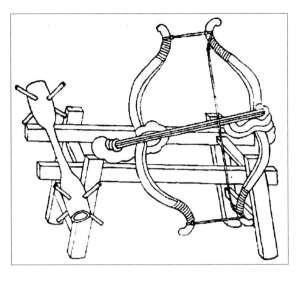

trigger mechanism alone was a masterpiece of precision engineering, while the bow itself was a composite reflex bow that combined layers of horn, bamboo and sinew into a powerful spring mounted on a strong stock. The siege crossbow was based on similar principles and used the same trigger mechanism, but was of a much larger size and was therefore mounted on some form of framework. Similar devices were known in the West from antiquity, and large crossbows called 'gastraphetes', firing suitably large arrows, are first recorded during the siege of Syracuse in 399 BC. The Hellenistic mounting was typically a static tripod, although Chinese varieties could also be fitted to a wheeled carriage.

Two other important features were associated with the Chinese siege crossbow. The first was the development of a model that could shoot several arrows at once. In an account of 120 BC we read:

'The soldiers of these late times have had to be equipped with battering rams for attack, and shields against the arrows; they shoot with multiple-bolt crossbows which are lashed to carriages for the fight.'

The other development was the incorporation of one or two extra bowstaves into the construction to increase the energy of tension. This latter variety was also probably used for multiple-bolt firing, so there was a certain degree of overlap between the two types.

An early account of 99 BC tells of large crossbows mounted on carriages forming a 'laager' against a mounted attack, and for the next 1,200 years heavy crossbows were an accepted feature of Chinese siege warfare. The earliest description of a crossbow designed specifically for the defence of city walls occurs in the writings associated with the name of Mo Zi and dates from c.380–350 BC. His crossbows were massive weapons built on a four- or six-wheeled framework on a double axle from timbers one foot square and operated by a crew of ten men. The carriage stood eight feet off the ground and fired arrows ten feet long, which projected three feet in front of the bow on a stock of six feet. The bow was drawn by a winch using 'left and right claws', the only practical way of arming such a monster. It could be raised or lowered on to a target and was fitted with sights. When the large arrow was released, several smaller bolts were fired off with it, and it is interesting to note that the large arrows (of which 60 were issued to each bow) had ropes fitted to them like a harpoon and were pulled back by windlass for further use.

The range of this early weapon is not given, but later versions used during the Tang dynasty

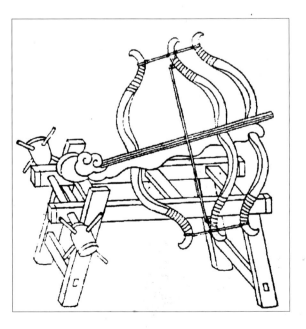

BELOW **A triple-bow crossbow of the Song dynasty mounted on a static frame. As in the accompanying example, no details of the arming mechanism other than the winch handles are given. A possible reconstruction of the stringing arrangement is given in Plate D. (Japan Archive)**

are said to have attained a maximum range of 1,160 yards. This amazing range is actually supported by a Persian source describing the use of similar machines fired from a position on the top of a mountain during the Mongol attack on one of the castles of the Assassins in 1256. The normal operating range of a single-bow siege crossbow would be between 270 and 500 yards. Up to a certain distance, the bolts were armour piercing; these weapons were much feared because of their penetrating power.

From the basic siege crossbow evolved several variations including even larger versions, with size limited solely by width of the walkway of the walls on which they were usually mounted. About AD 300, a commentator noted similar crossbows being armed by oxen rather than a winch, although this may be a merely figurative expression of the force needed akin to 'horse power'; in 759 we read of a Tang version with a stock 12 feet in length, which 'made a noise like thunder' when it was released.

The biggest variation comes with the missiles themselves, and the Tang account helpfully explains how it was possible to fire several arrows at once from one bowstring. Not surprisingly, the seven arrows described as being fired simultaneously are graduated in size, and lie in grooves prepared on the upper surface of the stock. The central arrow is three feet long, with a seven-inch iron head and iron tail fins. The range claimed for this machine is 700 paces (525 yards), within which range 'whatever is hit will collapse, even solid things like ramparts and city towers'. Further variations are noted in the literature, including the modifications introduced by one general who replaced the set of one large wooden arrow and progressively smaller bolts by ten iron bolts only eight inches long. On occasions, whole batteries of these machines could be linked together and operated from one central release. An account of such an arrangement described in about 950 calls the ensemble a 'rapid dragon engine'.

The other Chinese variety of siege crossbow incorporated a second or even a third bow on the framework to provide extra tension to the bowstring. This weapon, unknown in the Western world, may have originated at the same time as the multiple-bolt crossbow, although early descriptions are ambiguous, but it reached its heyday under the Song just before it was supplanted by gunpowder weapons. It was also used in Southeast Asia. In 1171, a Chinese official journeyed to Champa (Vietnam), where he stayed to teach horse archery and the use of crossbows. There are depictions of multiple-bow crossbows mounted on elephants and on two-wheeled carriages on carvings at Angkor Thom in Cambodia.

The most likely arrangement for stringing the double crossbow would be to have the ends of the string attached firmly to the rear bow and slipped freely over both ears of the forward one. This would enable it to be drawn by two ropes from a winch just as in the multiple-bolt example discussed above, and the Cambodian reliefs support this view. In illustrations of the triple-bow crossbow, the string is shown located on the middle bow, so the likely explanation is that it was attached to the forward bow and looped first over the rear bow and finally over the middle bow, as in Plate D.

The Mongol use of the siege crossbow

Great skill and experience is needed to operate weapons as complex as siege crossbows, as was indicated when the Mongol armies began to recruit large numbers of Chinese artillery engineers from the mid-thirteenth century onwards. In 1255, Mongke Khan's army included many 'shooters of fiery arrows worked by a wheel' – no doubt a reference to the siege crossbow's winch – 'worked in such wise that one bow string would pull three bows, each of which would discharge an arrow of three or four ells in length.' Mongke's machines also threw pots of naphtha, and were themselves fireproofed by being covered in hides. The Mongol cross-bows could be broken down into five or seven parts, and were transported on carts to the site of action. One thousand 'crews' of Chinese artillery-men accompanied Hulegu to the West and helped breach the walls of Baghdad in 1258.

During their campaigns against the Southern Song, the Mongols had Chinese siege machines used against them and it may well have been the multiple-bow cross-bow that produced a serious reverse in their fortunes. By 1259, Mongke Khan had pacified the whole of

A Japanese soldier of the Nara Period with a crossbow. The weapon shown here is too large to be held in the hand, and can probably be regarded as the smallest variety of the mysterious oyumi. (Japan Archive)

Sichuan. He then headed east and laid siege to Diaoyu, where resistance was so firm that Mongke abandoned the siege after six months. Other Mongol armies, including Mongke's brother Khubilai, then advanced in support, but just as Mongke was preparing to take the field again, he died, either from dysentery or from wounds inflicted by a Song siege weapon. His death gave the Southern Song a 20-year reprieve from Mongol attacks.

The siege crossbow in Japan

The crossbow was introduced to Japan from the Koguryo state in 618, when the Koreans delivered two Chinese prisoners of war and several pieces of military equipment. By 672, it was being used in warfare, with reports of crossbows shooting arrows 'just like rain', an expression that may imply multiple-bolt crossbows rather than hand-held ones, although both are known to have been manufactured in Japan. A Japanese artisan called Shimaki no Fubito Makito had even succeeded in improving upon the Chinese crossbow by 835, producing 'a frontier weapon' that 'can be shot from four direction; it rotates and is easy to set off', a description that is not unlike that of the Hellenistic tripod-mounted siege crossbows. In 838, the government of Mino province ordered four of the new machines to replace 20 of the old issue. During the 860s, the Japanese government were concerned over a possible invasion from the Korean state of Silla, and placed crossbows in a number of possible landing sites on the Sea of Japan coast. There was a battle in 894 between Japanese and Korean ships, during which crossbows were used. Whether these were hand held or large varieties is not clear, but 29 static crossbows and 100 hand-held ones were among the plunder taken when rebels seized and burned Akita in northern Japan.

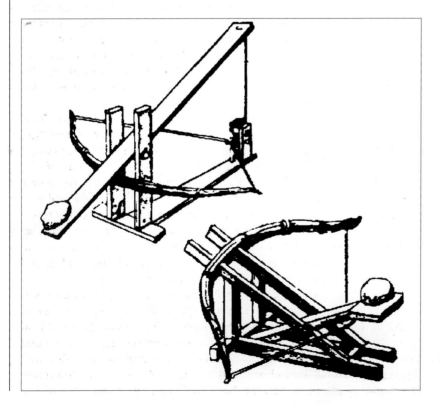

Two varieties of Japanese stone-throwing crossbows as reconstructed by Sasama. Both are practical, but it may be that the addition of a small sling to an ordinary oyumi was all that was needed to convert it from an arrow-firing machine, as these siege weapons were used as anti-personnel weapons rather than for breaking down walls. (Japan Archive)

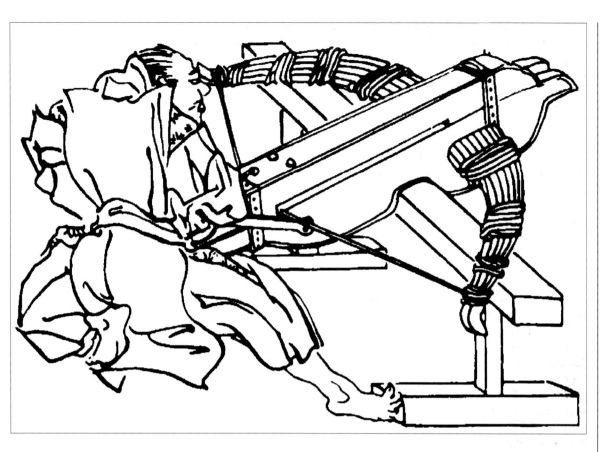

Another possible design of an oyumi. This is larger than the previous example. Reliable sources also speak of Japanese crossbows being mounted on 'universal joints' on wooden stands. (Japan Archive)

As no Japanese oyumi (siege crossbow) has survived, it is impossible to know exactly what one looked like or how it was operated. Certain records make tantalising reference to them being different from Chinese varieties, although this may just be an expression of national pride. It is, however, well substantiated that, in contrast to the predominant Chinese practice, the Japanese crossbows were used for throwing stones as much as for firing arrows.

In the *Mutsu waki*, the chronicle of the 'Early Nine Years' War' (1053–62) the use of both arrows and stones is recorded, where 'the assembled oyumi fired throughout the day and night, the arrows and stones falling like rain'. Stones are also implied by the use of the alternative expression ishiyumi (literally 'stone bow') that is frequently encountered for the crossbow. In the *Gosannen Kassen Ekotoba*, which is concerned with the 'Later Three Years' War' (fought, with periods of truce, between 1083 and 1089) the hero, Ban Jiro Kenjo Sukekane, is struck on the helmet by a stone from an ishiyumi and knocked to the ground. In the *Oshu Gosannen ki*, which covers the same conflict, we also read of the existence of 'a siege weapon' that fired stones from a castle wall.

The use of crossbows, with their technological sophistication and need for expertise in their operation, gradually declined in Japan in favour of mounted archers wielding longbows. There was also a political factor involved, because the resources of a centralised state were needed to maintain crossbow manufacture and use, as central authority declined through the Heian Period so did the reserve of trained crossbowmen. Crossbow adepts soon became hard to find, and at the time of the

Hogen Rebellion in 1156 a certain Kiheiji Taifu was praised by his master, Minamoto Tametomo, for being 'one who can throw stones three cho' (about 350 yards).

The swansong of the Japanese siege crossbow would appear to be 1189, when Minamoto Yoritomo led an army to the far north of Japan in pursuit of his brother, Minamoto Yoshitsune, and his Fujiwara allies. When Yoritomo attacked a fortress near Mount Atsukashi, he took 18 heads in spite of many deadly shots from crossbows but from this time on references to Japanese crossbows disappear from the record. To some extent this was due to the fact that, with the notable but short-lived exceptions of the Shokyu War of 1220 and the Mongol invasions, the thirteenth century in Japan was a time of almost unbroken peace, giving ample opportunity for such a specialist skill to be lost completely.

CATAPULT SIEGE ARTILLERY

The Traction Trebuchet in China

The alternative to throwing stones by crossbow was to use torsion catapults of twisted sinew (a machine never adopted in the Far East) or varieties of the pivot catapult, or trebuchet, of which the earliest and simplest used manpower as the motive force. This latter type, the traction trebuchet, became the backbone of Chinese siege artillery. Known in the West as the 'perrier' or petraria' (the term 'trebuchet' being reserved for the counterweight variety), the traction trebuchet was able to deliver heavier payloads than a stone-firing bow, but over a shorter distance.

The Chinese traction trebuchet is at least as old as the siege crossbow and is also described in the Mo Zi writings. Once again, the descriptions are somewhat vague, but the basic design can be described as follows. The catapult consisted of a wooden frame standing 13 feet above ground, but a further four feet may have been buried in the ground for stability. The pivot was made from the wheels and axle of a cart, round which swung a long throwing arm made from several timbers lashed together. The arm was up to 35 feet long, three-quarters of which was above the pivot and a quarter below, to which the pulling ropes were attached. The sling carried by the projectile was two feet eight inches long. Stones or simple incendiaries were used as ammunition.

From the Qin and Han dynasties onwards, traction trebuchets were a common feature in sieges, both for attack and defence, and some were mounted on wheels. The defeat of the Sui dynasty by the Tang in 617 was achieved with the help of 300 trebuchets. When the Tang invaded Korea in 666, P'yongyang fell after a month-long siege involving trebuchets. A century later, trebuchets mounted on wheeled carriages were

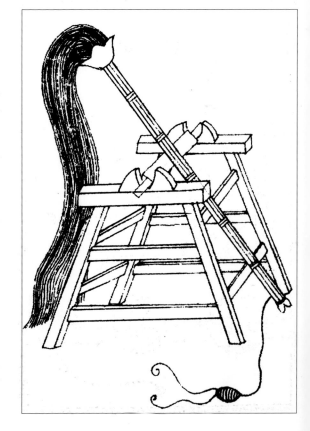

A 'four-footed trebuchet', the largest version of the Chinese traction trebuchet. Early texts imply that the legs were sunk into the ground to give stability. (Japan Archive)

used to quell a rebellion and were said to have required a team of 200 men to pull each of them.

A Tang dynasty description from 759 is very similar to that from Mo Zi, but includes references to 'whirlwind trebuchets' and 'four-footed trebuchets', two variations that are illustrated in the *Wu Jing Zong Yao* of 1044. The frame of the whirlwind trebuchet was a single vertical pole that could be rotated horizontally through 360 degrees, thus allowing a wide arc of fire for comparatively lightweight missiles. Another picture in the same source shows a whirlwind trebuchet mounted on a four-wheeled carriage, which would make it even more flexible. The 'four-footed trebuchet' was a larger and sturdier machine for heavier stones, apparently little different from the Mo Zi description.

Trebuchets played an important role in the fighting between the Southern Song and the Jin. Whirlwind trebuchets firing clay balls which would fragment on landing are specifically mentioned in the list of 114 Song siege machines installed on or behind the walls of Xiangyang in 1206 ready for an attack by the Jin. The Song also installed siege crossbows. The commander having been reliably informed that these were the weapons that the Jin feared most, he increased the number of crossbowmen by 3,000. The following year the Jin laid siege to the much-disputed De'an, and in a demonstration of psychological warfare, killed their Song prisoners and threw dozens of their severed heads back into the city using trebuchets.

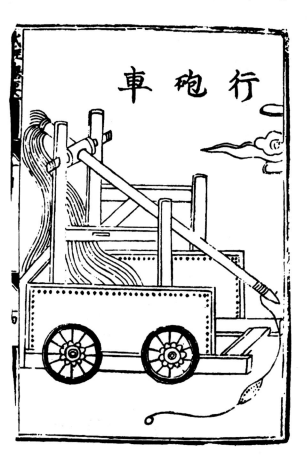

A traction trebuchet of the Song dynasty mounted on a simple mobile carriage. (Japan Archive)

車砲行

The mode of operation of a traction trebuchet appears in the writings of Chen Gui, who states that catapults should not be placed upon a city's walls, but should fire from the ground below, with a soldier placed on the wall as an 'artillery observer'. For a small difference in direction the hauliers need only move their feet. For a larger change, the whole machine should be moved unless it is of the simpler whirlwind type. Range is determined by how hard the ropes are pulled, so to shorten the distance men are taken out of the crew, and to increase it more men are added. Large trebuchets are best for use against enemy machines, and lighter ones with a long range for picking out small, individual targets such as enemy generals.

Until the introduction of the counterweight trebuchet in 1272, the motive power was provided by a group of hauliers pulling strongly and in unison, and there is still some controversy over how this was done. The reference noted above to teams of 200 men implies a gang who would be very likely to get in each other's way, although an alternative understanding of the 'team' could be a system that rotated its hauliers. This would allow them to rest from the very significant effort involved in projecting stones, and would lose none of the advantage of the very short time needed for a traction trebuchet to be reloaded and re-set. Unlike the counterweight trebuchet, which had to be cranked laboriously back into its ready position, a simple downward pull on the firing side of the arm was all that was needed.

In Caerphilly castle in Wales there is a reproduction traction trebuchet, and experiments have shown it can lose six stones a minute. The Caerphilly trebuchet also provides useful information about the likely position adopted by the hauling team, because the modern crew simply pulls almost vertically downwards on the ropes, with satisfactory results. This is the position suggested by medieval Western illustrations of traction trebuchets in illuminated manuscripts, in which the group usually consists of about half a dozen hauliers standing directly under the arm of the machine; an identical arrangement is found in the Central Asian source depicted in the accompanying illustration.

Chinese drawings of the machines, however, often show a very large number of pulling ropes, which would be totally impractical if the hauliers had to stand close together and pull downwards as one. It is probably for this reason that two recent reconstructions of traction trebuchets, painted by Japanese artists, have favoured an arrangement whereby the pulling ropes are passed under the frame of the trebuchet and are pulled in an almost horizontal direction by the hauliers. In the absence of any contemporary illustration of Chinese traction trebuchets actually being fired, it is impossible to decide which of the assumptions is the correct one. However, the 'horizontal' method would certainly allow more hauliers, and if the crossbeam was correctly placed there should be little loss of mechanical advantage. It may well be the case that there was something of a compromise between the two in the case of large trebuchets, with the team spread out wide, using long ropes. This is supported to some extent by an important Western source: a thirteenth-century carving of a traction trebuchet where some members of the team are pulling horizontally.

This same carving also shows that the force of the hauliers is being supplemented by the addition of a heavy weight. It is interesting to note that when the Jin defended Luoyang against the Mongols in 1232 they appear to have done the same, so that 'few men were needed to work it, yet great stones could be hurled more than 100 paces, and there was no target which it did not hit right in the middle'. This would make it an intermediate stage between the traction and the counterweight trebuchet. It may be that the use of a much smaller crew was an important stimulus towards the development of the counterweighted machine, because the large number of hauliers of a traction trebuchet operating in such close proximity must have been an inviting target for 'counter-battery fire', either from enemy trebuchets or multiple-bolt crossbows.

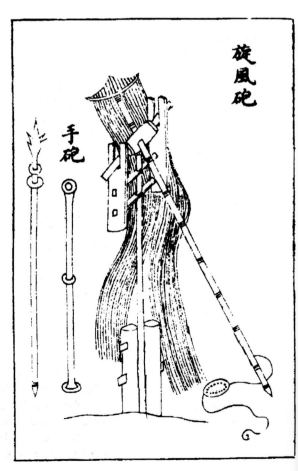

A whirlwind trebuchet, the arm of which could be rotated through 360 degrees. This was used for lighter projectiles, particularly when carrying out precision target shooting. (Japan Archive)

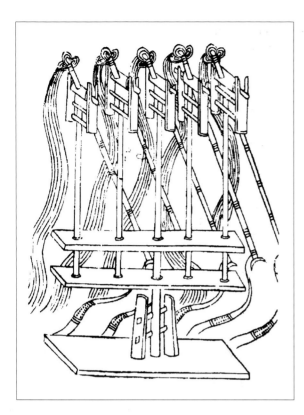

A battery of whirlwind trebuchets mounted on a single frame. (Japan Archive)

The Mongol Traction Trebuchet

As we saw with the siege crossbow, the Mongols rapidly adopted Chinese siege weapons when the situation demanded it. On one occasion, the reports of the Mongols' newly acquired prowess with trebuchets ensured that the inhabitants of a city targeted for attack not only laid waste the countryside for four or five miles around, but also carefully removed every stone they could find so that they could not be used as catapult ammunition. There was a similar shortage of stones during another campaign. We are not told if this was deliberate, but the Mongol artillerymen used balls of mulberry wood instead, hardened by soaking them in water. The Mongols made extensive use of traction trebuchets during their campaigns in Korea, notably at the sieges of Kuju and Chukju. The defenders of Kuju met fire with fire, matching the Mongol trebuchets with similar machines of their own. In the long account of the siege of Kuju, we read that 'the Mongols then attacked the south wall of the city with 15 large catapults very quickly. Pak So also constructed platforms on the city walls and, mounting catapults on them, he hurled stones and drove the attackers off.' A later section illustrates how traction trebuchets were capable of being aimed at a specific target:

'(General Kim) Kyong-son leaned against a light chair to direct the fighting. A Mongol catapult slung a missile across the wall and it hit directly behind Kyong-son, smashing and breaking the heads and bodies of the guards. Everyone begged Kyong-son to move the chair. Kyong-son told them, "That would not be proper. If I am to move, then the hearts of all the soldiers will move also."'

As the siege continued, although the Mongols arranged 30 catapults in a line and breached the wall in 50 places, as soon as the walls were smashed, the defenders tied iron chains across the breaches and quickly repaired the damage. Fierce counter-battery fire went on, and we may easily envisage both sides collecting unbroken catapult missiles and throwing them back against their opponents, perhaps doing this several times over.

During the 1235 invasion, another Mongol army laid siege to the sansong of Chukju. This stone and wood castle on a wooded hill provided a different challenge from Kuju, although accounts of the siege make it sound like Kuju in miniature, with much use being made of traction trebuchets on both sides. Korea was finally vanquished in 1273, suffering the indignity of having its entire navy requisitioned for Khubilai Khan's first attempt at an invasion of Japan. It was almost certainly traction trebuchets that threw the famous exploding bombs used during the Mongol landing in 1274, although whether they were launched from aboard the ships or on the beaches is not known. The need for portability in a naval operation strongly suggests that the lighter whirlwind catapults would have been used in Japan.

The Traction Trebuchet in Japan

It is beyond doubt that the Mongol exploding bombs were the first weapons of their kind used in Japan. Can the same also be said of the traction trebuchets by which they were fired? The Japanese would almost certainly have come across them in Korea early in the seventh century during one of their expeditions as allies of the Paekche state. However, unlike the crossbows that were used as anti-personnel weapons, there does not appear to be any record of trebuchet use in Japan, simply because the siege situation did not demand it. Also, as noted earlier, the Shokyu War and the Mongol invasions were the only major disruptions to a time of peace in Japan that lasted from 1189 to 1331. Thus, it is perhaps not surprising to find an absence of references to any form of large projectile device, including the now-forgotten siege crossbows, during this time.

The celebrated exploits of Kusunoki Masashige made the Nanbokucho Wars (the 'Wars Between the Courts'), which lasted until 1392, into something of a golden age of siege warfare in Japan. Yet, once again, these operations were conducted against isolated fortresses rather than walled towns, and, although the sieges of Akasaka and Chihaya involved certain siege machines that are compared in the *Taiheiki* to devices of Chinese origin, there is no specific mention of either catapults or crossbows. There are, however, several references in war reports and casualty lists to samurai being killed or wounded by stones. For example, from an account of 1341:

A whirlwind trebuchet mounted on a four-wheeled carriage. This would give considerable mobility to the weapon. (Japan Archive)

'Item, the flag bearer Hikojiro, at the time of the battle of the fifteenth day of the same month, received a stone from Horigiri [castle] and because it broke his head he died.'

In various reports dating from 1333 onwards, we read of 'the flag bearer Nakabira struck at the base of the right eye by a stone', and another being hit on the shoulder by a stone as he broke into a certain castle. Another flag bearer is hit in the face 'leaving him half dead and half alive'; a dramatic expression also applied to a samurai struck on the head while he was destroying the water supply of Kaseta castle. Nor are these activities confined to central Japan. In 1372, one of the Shibuya families fighting in distant Kyushu was 'struck by a stone on the helmet so that he fell into the moat and died'.

It may well be that the stones were simply dropped from the castle walls, an impression strengthened by the fact that so many of the victims were flag bearers, who traditionally would be the first to approach the

虎蹲砲

The 'crouching-tiger' trebuchet of the Song dynasty. This is essentially an intermediate-sized version of traction trebuchet, and has a simple but rigid triangular frame. (Japan Archive)

enemy defences. It is not until 1468 that we find an unambiguous reference to the use of traction trebuchets in Japan. This was during the Onin War of 1467–76, by which time relations with China had been re-established under the Ashikaga. Trade with China was encouraged, and Japanese swords became a major export item, making a fresh wave of transmission of traction trebuchet technology from China to Japan very likely. In the *Hekizan Nichiroku* we read:

'A craftsman from Yamato province came to the camp and constructed hassekiboku [flying stone machines]. At the place where the stones hit their mark they broke completely into fragments. The siege machines threw stones and devices like Chinese plums. The operators threw loads of stone or destroyed armies by spreading fire within their ranks. The strategy for these machines' operation was to shoot stones of 12 kin [16 lb] in weight. They went about 300 paces.'

Each trebuchet had a crew of 40 men. The 'Chinese plums' were the soft-cased exploding bombs described in Volume 2 of this work, and the statement about the range and limited size of the projectiles illustrates how backward Japan was in regard to artillery compared to contemporary China or Europe, where even the counterweight trebuchet, which was reaching the end of its useful life, was still capable of throwing stones 20 times heavier over the same distance. It is also interesting to note that the stones broke upon landing, a matter that caused the attackers no concern. It is likely that the trebuchet was being used as an anti-personnel weapon in the classic Japanese manner, rather than for creating a breach, for which stones of greater strength than their targets would be required. Records exist of similar methods being used on occasions by the Mongols, who sometimes fired clay balls as projectiles, the commentator adding that as they shattered on landing the defenders could not re-use them.

Sporadic accounts of stone-throwing catapults occur in the Japanese chronicles over the next two centuries, of which the most remarkable concerns the siege by the Mori family on the castle of Takigawa in 1552. The defenders had prepared for the assault by collecting large smooth stones from the river bed and bombarded the Mori forces with them, which, in the absence of evidence to the contrary, I assume was done by traction trebuchets rather than counterweight trebuchets. The most interesting feature of the siege is that after the attack the Mori leaders compiled the customary list of dead and wounded, and noted the weapons by which the wounds had been inflicted. The list includes casualties from catapult stones, a feature unique to this document, and they are so extensive that dropping stones by hand can be confidently dismissed as a means of delivery. Out of 181 men listed as wounded, 39 (22%) were wounded by edged weapons when the two armies came to grips, while the vast majority (78%) suffered wounds from missile weapons. Of these, 142 in total, 108 (76%) were wounded by arrows and 34 (24%) by trebuchet stones. In other words, the use of the traction trebuchet produced nearly a quarter of all wounds from missile weapons, showing that its effectiveness as an anti-personnel weapon could be quite considerable.

Another very detailed account of the use of stone-throwing catapults in Japan occurs in the Ou Eikei Gunki description of the siege of Omori in 1599. Omori, in the far north of Japan, was defended by a peasant army against an overbearing landlord, and their leader had 'skilfully made from brushwood [a term that probably means rough timbers] things for throwing stones. Used by women and children, they could easily project them about one cho (120 yards).' Such a range, which is about one-third of the distance the 40 footsoldiers of the Onin War could hurl their stones, is consistent with the machines being operated by untrained women and children, but the effect was no less devastating:

'Every single one of the two or three hundred women from inside the castle came out and began to throw down an abundance of large and small stones which they had already prepared, shouting as they defended, whereupon more than 20 men were suddenly hit and died. Many more were wounded. In fact, and regrettably, because of the women's act of opportunity in throwing stones, driven by necessity and scrambling to be first they jumped into the moat and fled outside the palisade. This treatment inspired those within the castle. [Then] about 20 arquebuses opened fire. This was not enough to frighten [the women], and the throwing of small stones from the shadows of the moat

The reproduction traction trebuchet at Caerphilly in action. This reconstruction is remarkably similar to Chinese descriptions, and its operation by hauliers pulling vertically downwards displays how the Chinese weapon is likely to have been handled. (Japan Archive)

A: Elephant-mounted and wheeled double-bow siege crossbows at Angkor, Cambodia 1177

B: Stone and arrow-firing siege crossbows at Atsukashi, Japan 1189

C: Mobile traction trebuchet with molten iron bombs at Kuju, Korea 1231

C

TRIPLE-BOW SIEGE CROSSBOW WITH GUNPOWDER FIRE ARROWS AT DANGTU, CHINA 1131

(see plate commentary for full details)

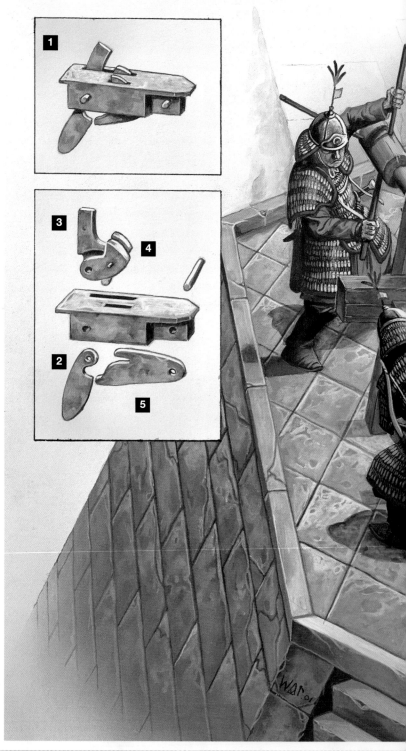

E: Counterweight trebuchet at
Xiangyang, China 1272

E

F: Fire oxen, fire balls and fire lances against siege towers at De'an, China 1132

G: Greek fire, naphtha incendiaries and gas bombs against shields and ladders at Kaifeng, China 1126

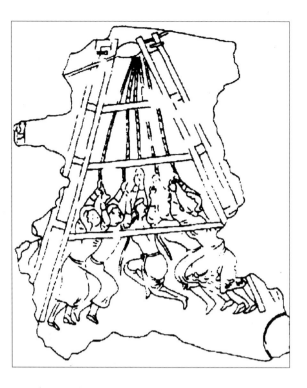

A fragment of a wall painting depicting the use of a traction trebuchet at the siege of Penjikent (700–725) in modern Tajikistan. This unique painting is contemporary with Tang China, displaying how the traction trebuchet was used along the Silk Road. Note how the hauliers are pulling downwards to fling their projectile. (Courtesy of Dr David Nicolle)

was like a hail storm. To the irritation of Shiyoshi, they struck Ishii Ukon Koremichi in both eyes and killed him. Similarly, they struck in one eye the horse that Kutsuzawa Goro was riding. Saying "to stay too long in that place and be hit by women's stones would be a failure bringing ridicule for generations to come", they returned to the original place of attack.'

The traction trebuchet thus continued to be used in Japan long after it had been abandoned in China and the West. A final reference to the use of catapults concerns the siege of Osaka castle in 1614 where, Sadler tells us in *The Maker of Modern Japan*, the defenders installed 'fire-projecting mangonels', for which traction trebuchets may best be understood. As it was during this action that the Tokugawa besiegers bombarded the castle from a long distance using European cannon, this remark tells us more about the paucity of artillery possessed by the defenders than about a reasoned application of defensive strategy.

The Counterweight Trebuchet

The counterweight trebuchet, in which the group of men pulling ropes were replaced by the force of a descending weight, was a very important development in siege artillery, soon replacing the traction trebuchet wherever it was introduced, even if the traction trebuchet still possessed the advantage of portability and speed. In both Europe and Asia the counterweight trebuchet was a huge, static monster, often constructed at the site of the siege itself, that pounded city walls to great effect. Yet 'the old type of trebuchet was really more convenient', said the founder of the Ming dynasty in 1388. 'If you have a hundred of these machines, then when you are ready to march, each wooden pole can be carried by only four men. Then when you reach your destination, you encircle the city, set them up, and start shooting.' Nevertheless, the greater range and weight of the projectile provided by the counterweight trebuchet was to make it the queen of siege warfare, and it is to this machine, the pinnacle of achievement of non-gunpowder artillery, that we now turn.

Of the date of the introduction of the counterweight trebuchet to China there can be no doubt. It occurred in 1272, during one of the greatest sieges of Chinese history, at Xiangyang, where the Mongols besieged the Southern Song for five years. Xiangyang (the present-day Xiangfan) was the same place that the Song had so valiantly defended against the Jin in 1206, and consisted of the twin cities of Xiangyang and Fancheng, which lay opposite each other across the Han River. They formed the northern outpost of the Southern Song, being their last bastion beyond the central basin of the Yangtze, withstanding the siege by Khubilai Khan from 1268 to 1274 while being defiantly supplied by riverboat. Even when a river blockade was finally put in place and firmly maintained, the Mongol siege weapons of traction trebuchets and siege crossbows proved incapable of causing any real damage to the twin cities and their walls.

Something stronger was needed, and this was supplied in the form of Muslim counterweight trebuchets and their operators, who were summoned to China from the lands of the West. It is interesting to note that the traction trebuchet had made its way from China to the West centuries earlier, and now it returned in a new and more terrifying form. The counterweight trebuchet had long been valued in Europe and the Middle East, having rapidly supplanted the traction trebuchet since its first recorded use in 1165. In 1291, 20 years after Xiangyang, its Muslim enthusiasts were to bring 92 counterweight trebuchets into action with devastating results against the crusader stronghold of Acre.

The actual design of these machines as they were used in China is by no means clear. The familiar image that we have in the West is that of a trebuchet for which the counterweight appears in the form of a large bucket, like the scoop of a modern mechanical digger, which is able to swing freely on the end of the arm. This version, however, was preceded by a model having a fixed counterweight, which was the natural first stage of the process of converting the 'weight-assisted' traction trebuchet noted earlier to the true counterweight version with no hauliers.

On examining the Chinese sources, a description of the siege of Xiangyang written 30 years afterwards tells us, 'When [the artillerymen] wanted to hurl them to a greater range, they added weight [to the counterpoise] and set it further back [on the arm]; when they needed only a shorter distance, they set it forward, nearer [the fulcrum].' This description of an adjustable counterweight is supported by a crude drawing of a mobile version in which the counterweight is shown fastened to the arm by a rope, and would therefore have acted as a primitive form of swinging counterweight. It is also interesting to note that the trebuchets are described as being mounted 'above holes in the ground', which probably means that the frame was sunk into the ground for stability as in the Mohist example.

There is, however, an intriguing passage from the Southern Song side of the conflict, because in response to the Mongol advance the Song began making counterweight trebuchets of their own: 'In 1273 the frontier cities had all fallen [into the Mongols' hands]. But Muslim trebuchets were constructed with new and ingenious improvements, and different kinds became available, far better than those used before.' This could mean swinging counterweights more like the familiar European version, or the mysterious 'improvements' may simply refer to

A drawing of a thirteenth-century stone carving at the Church of Saint-Nazaire in Carcassonne that is believed to depict the siege of Toulouse in 1218. It shows a traction trebuchet, and illustrates two important points. First, some of the hauliers (who include a woman in their number) are pulling horizontally, a method that is implied by Chinese illustrations. Second, there is apparently a heavy weight on the pulling end of the beam to assist the effort, thus showing the transition of the traction trebuchet toward the full counterweight version with no hauliers. (Japan Archive)

a comparison with traction trebuchets, as it would indeed be strange if Khubilai Khan's imported engineers had not made use of the best machines at their disposal.

Whatever the details of their design, the Muslim trebuchets were constructed at the Yuan capital, where Khubilai Khan attended some of the trials in person, then transported to Xiang-yang. This may have been by dismantling the machines, although they could have been mounted on wheeled carriages. Projectiles weigh-ing ten times more than any stone hitherto fired could now be launched, and one particular shot (perhaps exceeding 200 lb) launched on target brought down the drum tower of Xiangyang with a noise like thunder. The above commentator wrote that 'the projectiles were several feet in diameter, and when they fell to the earth, they made a hole three or four feet deep'.

Realising the tremendous advantage that he now possessed, Khubilai Khan wasted no time in sending out these new weapons against the Southern Song capital of Hangzhou. Bayan, one of the most gifted of all Mongol leaders, was chosen to lead the advance. He crossed the Yangtze in January 1275 and met the Song forces in a series of battles in which the Mongol superiority in artillery made a decisive difference. Bayan went on to bombard and take Yangzhou, 'breaking down temples, towers and halls', and in spite of the Southern Song's own rapid adoption of the new weapons, they had not long left to reign. Bayan occupied one town after another, some surrendering as soon as the army came in sight, and finally Hangzhou fell.

The use of a four-footed traction trebuchet to fire thunderclap bombs during the Onin War in Japan in 1468. In this reconstruction, a pulling method using 40 men pulling horizontally has been adopted. (Illustration by Howard Gerrard from *Ashigaru* by the author in the Osprey Warrior Series)

The use of a Muslim counter-weight trebuchet as depicted in Raschid al Din's *World History*. Basic models similar to this were taken to China in 1272. (Japan Archive)

On completion of the conquest of the Southern Song in 1279, the newly created emperor Khubilai Khan of the Yuan dynasty of China turned his attentions once more towards Japan, and planned a second invasion for 1281. Bombs had been thrown against the Japanese in 1274, probably from traction trebuchets, but the newer counterweight trebuchets do not appear to have been included in the plans for the second invasion. When the commander of the fleet asked for technicians for Muslim trebuchets, his request was declined on the grounds that the machines were not suitable for naval warfare. However, when a further Mongol invasion of Japan was being planned between 1283 and 1285, the emperor appears to have changed his mind, and an engineer was commissioned to build counterweight trebuchets to support the landings. Technicians were also drafted to the project but, as the invasion was cancelled, what would have been a unique military experiment was never carried out.

The Mongol use of a Muslim counterweight trebuchet, from the Saray album. Illustrations of such machines are remarkably consistent in their depictions of a simple but sturdy triangular frame, a sling and a winch mechanism. (Japan Archive)

In China, the use of the 'Muslim trebuchet', often also called the 'Xiangyang trebuchet' after the place where it had made such a lasting impression, continued to be the main piece of heavy artillery in the armoury of the Yuan dynasty, and was still being used by their successors, the Ming, until the end of the fifteenth century. As late as 1480, there were still those prepared to argue that knowledge of the making of trebuchets should be preserved in government archives 'just in case', and prohibited to unauthorised persons. It is interesting to note that during that same year of 1480 one solitary trebuchet was constructed for the Knights of Rhodes to use in their successful defence against the Turkish siege. The machine did good service, and helped conserve the garrison's precious stocks of gunpowder. The final use of the trebuchet in Europe was probably the siege of Malaga in 1487. By way of contrast, Japan appears never to have adopted the counterweight trebuchet, making the leap direct from traction trebuchets to cannon, although even these saw little use until the very end of the age of the samurai.

INCENDIARY DEVICES

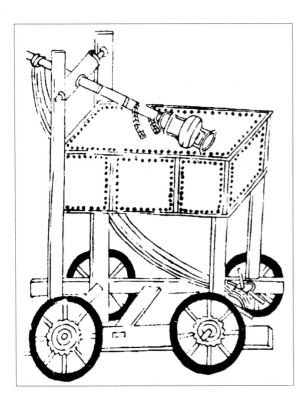

A Chinese wheeled counter-weight trebuchet of the Song dynasty. This rather strange illustration shows the machine ready to be moved. The counterweight box (presumably emptied of any rocks) has been supported on two uprights for security. (Japan Archive)

Siege artillery, whatever the means of propulsion used, had as its aim the destruction of an enemy's walls, houses, gates or siege engines, and if this could not be done by breaking them down with stone, then some method of incendiary warfare was a popular alternative. In this section we will examine the incendiary devices that either preceded the introduction of gunpowder or made limited use of its chemical properties. The simplest incendiaries of all were the 'pheasant-tail torches', bundles of dry straw and other material shaped like the letter 'Y', soaked in fat and wax, with spikes to enable them to stick to the roofs of assault vehicles. The arms of the 'Y' fell naturally over the roof beam of a cart.

Fire Arrows

One activity for which the large siege crossbow was admirably suited was the shooting of fire arrows. As early as 229, a certain besieging army saw their battering rams and scaling ladders burned by fire arrows, and in 535 all the siege engines of another attacking army were similarly destroyed. In 994, Northern Song trebuchets fired stones while crossbows shot fire arrows to drive off a siege by the Liao. In all these examples, the actual incendiary material was probably some form of mineral oil, perhaps with sulphur added. A Tang source of 759 describes a two-stage process for an incendiary attack whereby arrows to which gourds of oil had been attached were first fired into a city. These broke on landing, spreading the oil on to the roofs of houses. Fire arrows, probably carrying burning tow (hemp fibres), then followed, setting the roofs alight.

By the eleventh century, gunpowder had arrived; a description of a triple-bow siege crossbow and its ammunition includes the words 'to all these bolts one can add gunpowder, but the amount, whether heavy or light, much or little, will depend on the strength of the catapult'. The result of 'adding gunpowder' at this stage in history was not to create an explosion as such but to produce an incendiary device that was picturesquely named 'the fiery pomegranate arrow shot from a bow'. The description that follows refers to the variety loosed from a hand-held bow, although those used with the siege crossbow cannot have been very different:

'Behind the arrow-head wrap up some gunpowder with two or three layers of soft paper, and bind it to the arrow shaft in a lump shaped like a pomegranate. Cover it with a piece of hemp tightly tied, and sealed fast with molten pine resin. Light the fuse and then shoot it off from a bow.'

In 1131, these weapons were included in a formidable armoury when a unit of Southern Song troops were besieged in Dangtu by the Jin. By means of gunpowder fire arrows, Greek fire projectors and traction trebuchets, the Song succeeded in destroying all the attacking enemy's wooden scaling ladders and siege works.

Incendiary Bombs

As noted in the account immediately above, trebuchets were another obvious means of delivering incendiaries, and simple 'fire balls', mostly using low-nitrate gunpowder as an incendiary material, were made to be hurled from trebuchets into the enemy lines. The 'igniter fire ball' used wax as the combustible mixture; because it would burn for some time it was designed to be fired before any other incendiary projectile and thus acted as a range finder for subsequent incendiary bombs. There was also the 'barbed fireball' that had a series of hooks on its outer surface. The ball was ignited before throwing and the hooks would ensure that it clung to whatever it struck. A similar device called the 'bamboo fire kite' ('kite' in the sense of the species of bird) was made from a bamboo basket weighted with stones and filled with gunpowder.

An alternative incendiary substance was molten iron. Ceramic containers were filled with molten iron and thrown from trebuchets, and this could have an incendiary effect if the bombs hit a wooden structure. The high phosphorus content of Chinese cast iron gave it a comparatively low melting point, so when used in the defence of cities it was melted in mobile furnaces that could be dragged along the walkways of the city walls. When Kaifeng fell to the Jin in 1126, the inventory of captured siege equipment included '20,000 fire arrows and a model of the trebuchet for hurling projectiles filled with molten metal'. Trebuchets hurling molten iron were a feature of Kim Kyong-son's defence of the Korean city of Kuju against the Mongols in 1231, and the Mongol general Bayan used molten-iron bombs fired from trebuchets at Yingcheng in 1280.

The Mongol campaigns in Korea also provide two illustrations of the use of incendiaries based on human fat. This was a bizarre, and one may assume, vastly inferior alternative to the Mongols' use of naphtha for similar purposes. We read that during the siege of Kuju in 1231:

'The Mongols soaked faggots with human fat, accumulated many of them, then attacked the city with fire. When Pak So tried to put them out with water, the fire burned more fiercely. He had his men mix mud of earth and water and throwing it on the fires extinguished them.'

Human fat was apparently used again at the siege of Chukju in 1236, and in 1275 Bayan is said

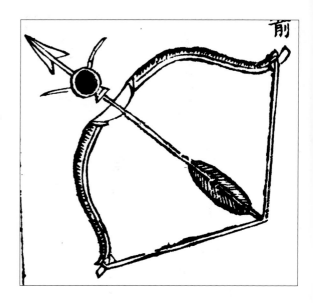

The so-called 'fiery pomegranate shot from a bow', a gunpowder-based incendiary arrow of the Song dynasty. Versions existed for both hand-held bows and siege crossbows. (Japan Archive)

A pheasant-tail torch, used for setting fire to siege weapons. The 'Y' shape was designed to allow it to be dropped on to the roof of an assault vehicle where it would stay until the fire spread. (Japan Archive)

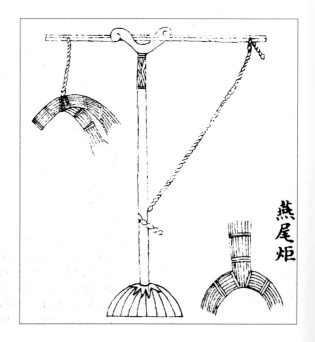

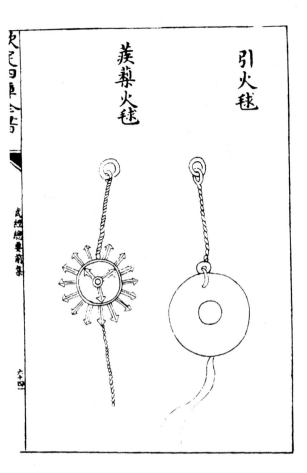

武經總要前集

蒺藜火毬　　引火毬

六十四

The barbed fireball, an incendiary bomb thrown by traction trebuchet, having spikes around its outer surface to enable it to stick to whatever target it hit. (Japan Archive)

to have used human fat against the Southern Song in missiles that were presumably thrown by trebuchets. Having killed and burned his captives, he 'used the boiling fat of the corpses to manufacture fire missiles which were thrown to set alight the wooden chevaux de frise of the wall battlements'. The fat may have been mixed with naphtha or some other petroleum-derived substance, but another account says merely that Bayan used human fat to lubricate his siege engines.

There are also several historical references to incendiary bombs filled with petroleum-based substances derived from the natural crude oil seepages that were known in China from 500 BC onwards. One account of the oil's sources says that 'there oozes out a liquid looking like uncoagulated fat. When burnt, it generates an intense brightness, but it cannot be consumed as food,' and all descriptions remark on how it cannot be extinguished using water. A lighter, lower boiling point fraction, obtained by filtration of the crude oil through fuller's earth, was to become known as naphtha. In 1253, when Hulegu Khan was setting off on the conquest of Persia, he sent to China for 'a thousand men skilled in war machines, naphtha throwing and crossbow shooting'. The naphtha was propelled from the catapults to its target in breakable ceramic pots, and at the end of the thirteenth century we come across a description of grenades containing naphtha (here referred to as 'mud oil') being thrown by hand in naval warfare:

'Four men hoist up the mud-oil into the crow's nest. Little bottles are filled with it, and a roll of betel-nut husk is used as a stopper. When this is lit it acts like a fuse. Then the bottles are thrown down from on high, and when the mud oil [bottles] hit the deck they [break and] burst into flames which spread everywhere and continue to burn.'

Animal-based Delivery Systems

In addition to being fired from crossbows or catapults, incendiary devices, and even the exploding bombs described in Volume 2, could be delivered to the enemy by the bizarre practice of fixing them to an animal and sending the terrified beast in the general direction of the foe. The simplest was the use of 'fire birds', which literally were birds. The wretched creatures had a walnut-size receptacle filled with burning tinder, pierced with two holes, tied around their necks. The idea was that they would settle on the roofs of an enemy's city and set fire to the thatch. Other versions have the containers tied to the birds' legs. One can only speculate what the reaction might have been should the birds decide to settle on the besiegers' own camp instead. A colourful story of the use of expendable animals is told concerning the Mongol siege of

Ningjiang in Manchuria in 1214. The besiegers promised to lift the siege if they were given all the cats and swallows in the town. As soon as these were delivered, lighted wool was fastened to their tails and they were let loose to burn the place down.

On occasions, much larger animals were used, producing the most remarkable siege weapon of all: the fire ox, which was a maddened ox with two spears attached to its sides and a burning incendiary on its rump. Alarming as it may sound, the approach of a fire ox may not have caused that many problems, as it was an easy target for an archer, and the incendiary device could be extinguished as soon as the animal was brought down. It may even have been regarded as a welcome addition to the victims' food supplies. But the later variant, where the fire ox carried a delayed-action exploding bomb on its back, was another matter. An actual description of one comes from an account of the Jin siege of De'an in 1132, where the Song successfully defended their city using fire lances and also one of the expendable animals described above:

'Gui, with sixty men, carrying fire lances, made a sally from the West Gate, and using a fire ox to assist them, burnt the flying bridges, so that in a short time all were completely destroyed.'

Apart from possibly destroying a soft target such as a scaling ladder or a siege tower, an exploding ox would also be an early example of chemical or biological warfare. The throwing of animal carcasses to spread disease is commonplace in siege descriptions from both Europe and Asia, and we have already noted the practice of throwing prisoners' severed heads back into a city, an activity that would have much more psychological than biological impact.

Greek Fire

Two Chinese siege devices spread fire by projecting flames rather than the throwing of incendiary bombs. The oldest form of flame projection used in China was the famous 'Greek fire', the 'secret weapon' of the Byzantine Empire, which entered the repertoire of Chinese siegecraft around 900. Unlike naphtha, Greek fire used petroleum that had been distilled, although many of the accounts of so-called naphtha-throwing in China (including the one quoted earlier) may also involve what was actually distilled petrol. The original Byzantine means of delivery was by siphons, which were effectively ancient flame-throwers, and this was adapted in China.

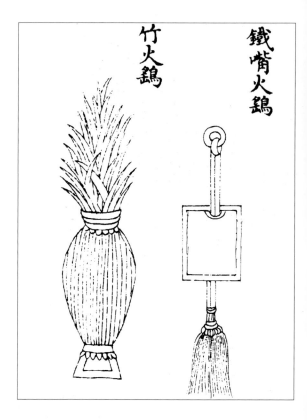

竹火鷂　　　鐵嘴火鷂

The 'bamboo fire kite' incendiary bomb, a simple device built around a basketwork container and thrown by traction trebuchet. (Japan Archive)

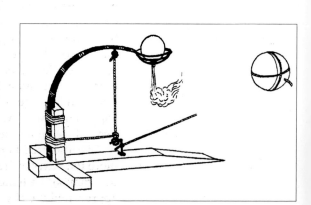

A Japanese bomb thrower that made use of the springy properties of bamboo. This was particularly favoured for naval warfare. (Japan Archive)

An expendable fire bird, which was a living bird fitted with incendiary material to be carried to an enemy's buildings. (Japan Archive)

A detailed description of the Chinese version is given in the *Wu Jing Zong Yao* of 1044, where it is interesting to note that the use of gunpowder for the ignition of Greek fire probably marks the first use of this vital substance in the history of warfare. The Greek fire container was made of brass, fitted with a horizontal pump that terminated in the gunpowder ignition chamber and a narrow-diameter nozzle. When the handle was pushed in and out vigorously petrol was squirted out. The author recommends placing these machines on the ramparts or the outworks of cities. When a town was attacked, rolls of blazing straw should first be thrown down on to the enemy's assault bridges. Burning petrol should then be sprayed on to them, and could not be put out with water.

An excellent account of the Chinese use of Greek fire concerns a battle on the Yangtze, near Nanjing in 975, between the Song and the Tang, where things did not quite go according to plan:

'The imperial [Song] ships were smaller but they came down the river attacking fiercely and the arrows flew so fast that the [Tang] ships were like porcupines. Zhu Lingbin hardly knew what to do. So he quickly projected petrol from flame-throwers to destroy the enemy. The Song forces could not have withstood this, but all of a sudden a north wind sprang up and swept the smoke and flames over the sky towards his own ships and men. As many as 150,000 soldiers and sailors were caught in this and overwhelmed, whereupon Lingbin, being overcome with grief, flung himself into the flames and died.'

A century later General Li Gang of the Song used Greek fire in an attempt to prevent the Jin from crossing the Yellow River before the siege of Kaifeng in 1126.

Fire Lances

The development of gunpowder allowed for another method of projecting flames. The fire lance or fire spear consisted of an ordinary spear to which was affixed a tube rather like a Roman candle. When lit by means of glowing tinder carried in a box at the soldier's belt, it burned for about five minutes, and when it was burned out its operator could use the spear for its conventional purpose. The fire lance was therefore a hand-held infantry weapon, but one that proved its real worth in a siege situation rather than on the battlefield, used in conjunction with a fire ox to burn siege ladders. The account of the 1132 siege of De'an tells us:

'We also used bomb gunpowder and long poles of bamboo to make more than twenty fire lances ... These things were got ready to use from the ramparts whenever the assault towers with their flying bridges approached the city.'

A century later, in the account of the siege of Kaifeng by the Mongols in 1232, we read that, in addition to the 'thunder crash bombs' to be described in Volume 2:

'... the defenders had at their disposal flying fire spears. These were filled with gunpowder, and when ignited flames shot forwards for a distance of more than ten paces, so that no one dared come near. These thunder crash bombs and flying fire spears were the only two weapons that the Mongol soldiers were really afraid of.'

Fire lances were also used during the siege of Xiangyang between 1268 and 1274 and as time went by these weapons grew more and more to resemble the hand-held guns that would eventually replace them, as pellets and arrows were discharged along with the flames, and certain varieties had metal barrels from as early as 1200. Fire lances 'shooting poisoned arrows' are mentioned during the second Mongol invasion of Japan in 1281. A century later, the picturesquely named 'sky filling smoke spurting tube', which discharged bits of broken porcelain, and the 'heaven

A fire ox, the most bizarre incendiary device of Song China. It has a blazing incendiary affixed to its rump. Later versions carried a delayed-action bomb. A fire ox (presumably the exploding variety) was actually used during the siege of De'an in 1132. (Japan Archive)

flying spurting tube', which added arsenic, were to be found belching smoke against Japanese pirate ships. The parallels are most striking when the fire lance came in the form of the 'fire tube', which was essentially a fire lance without the lance. One account of it, from 1220, makes it sound like a hand-held flame-thrower which burned for about five minutes.

In spite of their eventual transformation into, and replacement by, true firearms, the fire lance had a very long history of use as a siege weapon both in China and in the West. Fire lances were employed in Japan during the Onin War, and European versions are reliably recorded during the siege of Malta in 1565, and even as late as the siege of Bristol in 1643 during the English Civil War.

GAS BOMBS

Another early use of gunpowder in China was the smoke bomb and its more subtle variant called 'poisonous smoke bomb'. Their construction was ingenious. The bomb's inner core consisted of a substance that was largely gunpowder mixed with various poisons. It was made into a ball wrapped round many times with hemp string. The outer coating was a tinder based on moxa (a substance made from the mugwort plant), ignited by means of a red-hot brand just before it was shot off. The whole outer casing thus acted as a slow-burning fuse. The function of the gunpowder was not primarily to cause harm by exploding the device into fragments. Instead, the result of ignition of the inner gunpowder mixture was to produce, release and then spread vast clouds of toxic smoke. Descriptions of it refer to how it produced great discomfort among the enemy, causing bleeding from the mouth and nose.

Another variety of filling was composed almost entirely of human excrement mixed with various poisons, called the 'excrement trebuchet bomb'. The stoppered container holding the noxious mixture was flung from a traction trebuchet, and the results claimed for it, which include severe irritation and blistering, are said to derive from the fumes it produced. We may therefore assume that it was combined in some way with a gunpowder formula similar to the above mixture to create toxic smoke when it broke on landing. The catapult operators were recommended to chew black plums or liquorice as a protection against any leakage of poison. During the Yuan dynasty noxious explosive mixtures were combined in iron-cased fragmentation bombs.

The blinding effect of clouds of finely powdered lime was also utilised in catapult bombs. Lime was thrown in very fine and brittle earthenware containers, and formed just one item in the Song arsenal for defending their towns against the Jin in 1134:

'...the Jin soldiers erected towers at the river mouth in order to attack the city; but from its ramparts projectiles of molten iron were sent over, together with the jars of lime, and stones as well as arrows.'

A later account describes how the lime 'formed clouds of fog in the air, so that the rebel soldiers could not open their eyes.' The combination of lime with explosive bombs, another item in the Song repertoire, will be discussed in Volume 2.

COLOUR PLATE COMMENTARY

A: ELEPHANT-MOUNTED AND WHEELED DOUBLE-BOW SIEGE CROSSBOWS AT ANGKOR, CAMBODIA 1177

Multiple-bow siege crossbows are the only examples of large-scale Chinese weapons known to have been adopted in Southeast Asia. This plate depicts the attack on the Khmer capital of Angkor by King Jaya Indravarman IV of Champa (modern Vietnam) in 1177. The fall of the capital, which was defended only by wooden palisades, led to the occupation of Cambodia for the next four years, until the future Cambodian king Jayavarman VII staged a revolt and took the throne in 1181. The bas-reliefs at the Bayon of Angkor Thom, commissioned by the triumphant Jayavarman VII, depict battles between the Khmers over the Chams, and it is from these illustrations that the details of this plate are taken. We see two types of double-bow siege crossbows mounted on the backs of Vietnamese war elephants, an innovation introduced to Champa from China in 1171. Beside them is a double-bow siege crossbow mounted on a light wheeled carriage of a variety not seen in contemporary China. All three machines fire one large arrow at a time. The two insert diagrams show possible arrangements for stringing and arming the double-bow crossbows. The first is the simplest. Here the crossbow operates as a single-bow machine for releasing arrows. The rear bow, attached to the ends of the forward bow, is there merely to allow it to be armed by pulling back on the bow itself, thus slackening the string and allowing it to be looped over the trigger. The second diagram shows the system suggested by reliefs of the wheeled crossbow, and supported by Chinese sources, whereby the string passes over the forward bow and is attached to the ends of the second bow. A true 'two bow' system, it is armed by two men, who pull in unison using a double hook system.

B: STONE AND ARROW-FIRING SIEGE CROSSBOWS AT ATSUKASHI, JAPAN 1189

Japanese siegecraft was directed against isolated wooden fortresses in forested mountains rather than walled towns on the Chinese model. This meant that siege crossbows, known in Japan as oyumi, were used as large-scale anti-personnel weapons rather than primarily for destroying buildings. They fired both arrows and stones. This plate shows a typical wooden castle tower of an openwork construction augmented by movable wooden shields. It also attempts to reconstruct Japanese siege crossbows, of which no example has survived, from written descriptions of them and comparisons drawn from their Chinese counterparts. The context is the siege by Minamoto Yoritomo of a yamashiro (mountain castle) defended by the Fujiwara in 1189, the last occasion on which these weapons are known to have been used. Three varieties are shown. To the front is an arrow-firing oyumi, similar in design to a hand-held crossbow but just too heavy to be used by hand. This is based on a Chinese drawing which shows the string of the crossbow inside the frame. The one at the rear is being fired through a loophole in

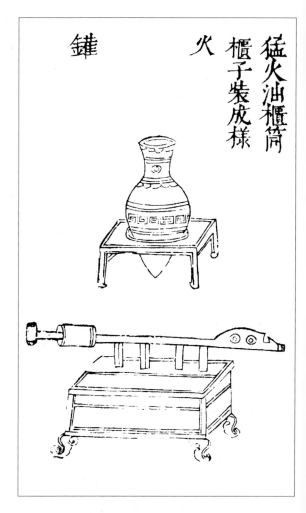

Details of a Greek fire projector, which the Song dynasty adopted from the Byzantine Empire. The burning petrol is squirted out by vigorously pumping the syphon handle. Commentators recommend throwing bales of burning straw on to the enemy by trebuchet, then pumping Greek fire on to the conflagration. (Japan Archive)

the tower and has been converted to project stones. The third variety has been mounted on to a swivelling wooden stand as described in the literature. It has been shown as a stand not unlike the ancient Greek versions, which enables it to be fired in any direction. Finally, a footsoldier lobs down a stone, the simplest method of defending a castle that is noted in Japanese chronicles over many centuries. There are several references in the literature to samurai and foot soldiers being wounded or killed by stones, but exact descriptions of how the stones were thrown, whether by hand or some sort of machine, are sadly lacking.

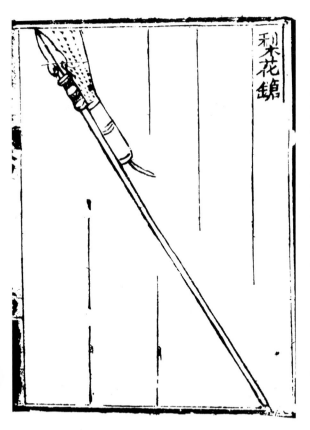

A fire lance or fire spear, a device much used in sieges, which had a considerable longevity in both Europe and the Far East. It consisted of a fire-projecting tube fixed just below the blade of a conventional spear. (Japan Archive)

C: MOBILE TRACTION TREBUCHET WITH MOLTEN IRON BOMBS AT KUJU, KOREA 1231

The traction trebuchet, a lever catapult of which the motive power was provided by a team of men pulling on ropes, was a very important Chinese siege weapon used by each of the four military cultures mentioned in this book. A particularly fierce exchange of traction trebuchet missiles marked the siege of Kuju, in what is now North Korea, by the Mongols in 1231. Stones, clay pots holding molten iron and incendiaries based on human fat were among the thousands of missiles flung by both sides. In this plate, we see the defenders of Kuju using a four-wheeled mobile version of a 'whirlwind' trebuchet to hurl molten iron bombs against the Mongol besiegers of Kuju. The fulcrum of the trebuchet is on a rotating pivot at the top of a single pole, that allows it to be aimed quickly and with some precision through 360 degrees. The ropes are pulled vertically downwards, and the huge pad formed by the coiled ropes acts as a cushion when the arm strikes the upright. In accordance with the recommendations of Chinese military writers, the trebuchet itself is firing from within the town, where a nearby forge supplies the molten iron bombs, while a senior Korean officer acts as an artillery observer from the walkway on top of the wall. Korean

descriptions indicate that the targeting achieved by a whirlwind trebuchet could be quite precise.

D: TRIPLE-BOW SIEGE CROSSBOW WITH GUNPOWDER FIRE ARROWS AT DANGTU, CHINA 1131

The siege crossbow was a mainstay of Chinese siege warfare for almost 1,500 years. Here we see a massive Song dynasty triple-bow siege crossbow mounted on a 12-foot stock stationed on the crossbow tower of the town of Dangtu during the siege by the Jin in 1131. Accounts tell us that these machines, together with Greek fire and traction trebuchets, succeeded in destroying all the Jin's wooden scaling ladders and siege works. The crewmen wind the bowstring back using a winch that pulls on either side of the bow against the enormous tension of the three compound bows. They are using iron bars slotted into the wooden frame. Another man stands by ready to put in place a large incendiary arrow called a 'fiery pomegranate gunpowder fire arrow'.

Cutaway drawings show the component parts and the operation of the complex bronze trigger system in the ready position and on release. The mechanism consisted of three interlocking levers mounted inside the housing (1). The rear one was the trigger (2). The central section, which shared the pivot pin with the trigger, was of double thickness, and had an extended rear lug on one side, usually the left, which acted as a sight, and may have been graduated for this purpose (3). Two projections at the front held the bowstring (4). The forward lever (5) rotated round a pin and engaged the central lever by means of a pin on that lever that slid between its jaws. Its own lower jaw was located into the trigger, where it was held in tension. When the trigger lever was pulled back, the two forward plates rotated to release the string.

The other inset diagram shows the probable method of stringing a triple-bow crossbow, whereby the arrow is located on the middle bow. The string passes over the middle and the rear bow in turn, and is anchored on the forward bow.

E: COUNTERWEIGHT TREBUCHET AT XIANGYANG, CHINA 1272

This plate shows the first use of the counterweight trebuchet in China, when Khubilai Khan's Mongols employed the expertise of Muslim engineers against the Southern Song during the siege of Xiangyang in 1272. As pictorial sources for these machines in China are almost non-existent, an attempt has been made to reconstruct their likely appearance using contemporary descriptions of machines at the siege of Xiangyang, a Song dynasty drawing of a mobile counterweight trebuchet, and several existing drawings of Mongol trebuchets in the Middle East and Central Asia, most of which agree surprisingly well on the main features. As the Muslims were the recognised experts in trebuchet manufacture during the thirteenth century it has also seemed reasonable to take details from the reliable near-contemporary European sources which have provided the basis for successful modern reconstructions of full-sized weapons. The Xiangyang trebuchet is therefore shown as a

神火萬全鐵圍管式

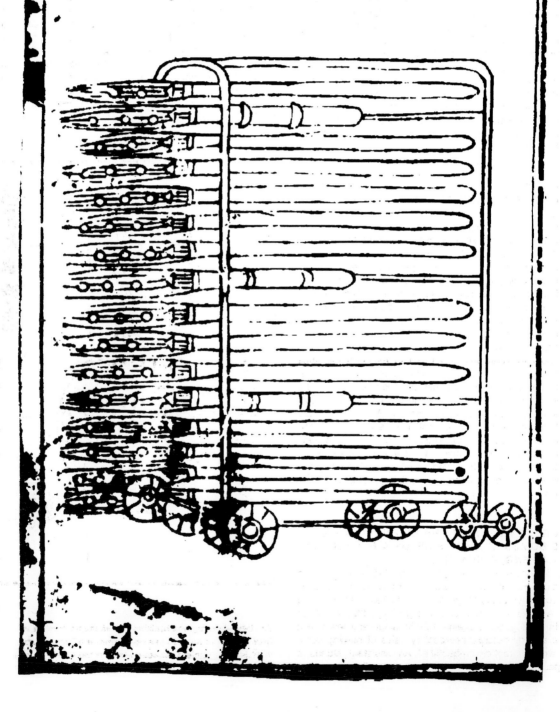

OPPOSITE A battery of fire lances. The fire lance is an ancestor of the gun. (Japan Archive)

large machine, but not impossibly so, brought to its firing position by a winch located under the sling end of the throwing arm. There is a straightforward iron trigger operated remotely by the simple expedient of hitting it with a mallet. The counterweight box is rectangular, as shown in the Song illustration, and provision has been made for it to be moved up and down the arm as described by a Chinese source, although presumably it would have to be unloaded first. The arrangement whereby the sling and projectile lie along a wooden trough is supported by reliable illustrations, and it has also been shown by modern experiments that adjusting the angle of the launching trough provides sufficient scope for aiming without having to move the entire trebuchet. For this reason, the upright timbers of the machine are sunk into the ground for stability, as noted in the contemporary Chinese source. As a final point of detail one of the crew is about to grease the joints using yak butter. In the distance a similar trebuchet is released, producing the same visual effect as that shown for trebuchets on most Muslim illustrations.

F: FIRE OXEN, FIRE BALLS AND FIRE LANCES AGAINST SIEGE TOWERS AT DE'AN, CHINA 1132

If one's enemy's siege weapons could not be smashed by catapult stones then they must be burned. In this plate, the Song defenders of De'an in 1132 are using three varieties of incendiary weapons against the besieging Jin, who have brought up a large mobile siege tower as a high platform for their crossbowmen to fire from. This machine receives barbed fireballs fired from traction trebuchets. The spikes on the outside of the fireballs have dug into the wooden supports of the tower and will stay in place until they have burned out. The Song have also made use of a fire ox. The unfortunate animal has been driven out of the gates in the general direction of the siege lines, with a delayed-action bomb on its back, and has exploded quite near to the siege tower. Another fire ox, but in this case carrying two spears and an incendiary, is on its way. Meanwhile, in the angle of the tower, more conventional resistance is offered against the Jin soldiers climbing up simple siege ladders by using a battery of fire lances. The sequence of events by which the fire lance is ignited, burns through as a flame-thrower and then becomes an ordinary spear is clearly shown.

G: GREEK FIRE, NAPHTHA INCENDIARIES AND GAS BOMBS AGAINST SHIELDS AND LADDERS AT KAIFENG, CHINA 1126

The defenders of the Song capital of Kaifeng in 1126 are seen using a wide range of siege weapons in their ultimately unsuccessful attempt to save their city from the advancing Jin. A Greek fire projector is being pumped vigorously to squirt blazing petrol against the Jin siege engines, which have already been bombarded by bales of burning straw thrown by traction trebuchets. An assistant stands a respectable distance away with further supplies of fuel. The

device at the end of the syphon tube contains the source of combustion, which was based on gunpowder. Naphtha grenades, which are thrown by hand against individual targets, are also used. Naphtha was a light fraction of crude oil obtained by filtration through fuller's earth. The grenades were of a ceramic substance fitted with a delayed action fuse. A brown stain on the shield of the Jin siege engine indicates the shattering of the ceramic container of a 'human excrement trebuchet bomb', which scatters its unpleasant contents around a wide area. It is probable that the dried human excrement was mixed with a form of gunpowder to spread the contents like a gas bomb. Undaunted, the Jin press forward with the simplest version of a cloud ladder. Its operators are protected as much as possible by a four-wheeled mobile shield, which a team of men controls so that it always hangs directly in front of the ladder. Further details of how a cloud ladder worked may be found in Volume 2. The hanging shield may have been made from treated leather to reduce weight. The details of Kaifeng are taken from a famous Chinese scroll-painting of the city finished the year before the city fell to the Jin.

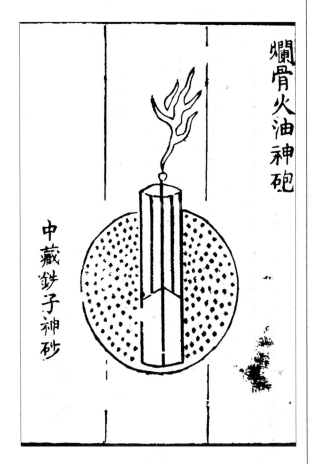

爛骨火油神砲

中藏鉄子神砂

The bone-burning and bruising fire-oil magic bomb, the final version of noxious gas bomb from the Yuan dynasty, combined its unpleasant contents with the explosion of a fragmentation bomb. (Japan Archive)

INDEX

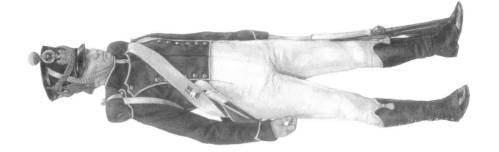

OSPREY
PUBLISHING

FIND OUT MORE ABOUT OSPREY

❑ Please send me a FREE trial issue
   of Osprey Military Journal

❑ Please send me the latest listing of Osprey's publications

❑ I would like to subscribe to Osprey's e-mail newsletter

Title/rank _____

Name _____

Address _____

_____

_____

Postcode/zip _____ state/country _____

e-mail _____

Which book did this card come from?

_____

❑ I am interested in military history

My preferred period of military history is _____

❑ I am interested in military aviation

My preferred period of military aviation is _____

I am interested in *(please tick all that apply)*

❑ general history ❑ militaria ❑ model making
❑ wargaming ❑ re-enactment

Please send to:

USA & Canada: Osprey Direct USA, c/o Motorbooks
International, P.O. Box 1, 729 Prospect Avenue, Osceola,
WI 54020

UK, Europe and rest of world:
Osprey Direct UK, P.O. Box 140, Wellingborough, Northants,
NN8 2FA, United Kingdom

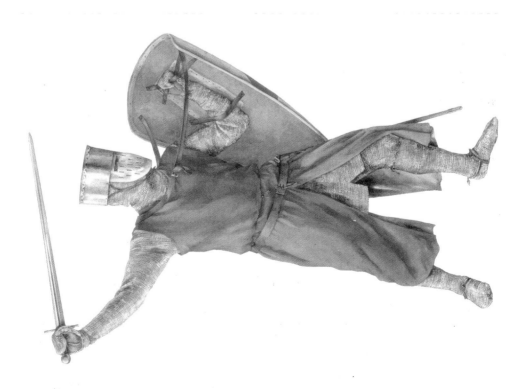

OSPREY
PUBLISHING

www.ospreypublishing.com

call our telephone hotline
for a free information pack

USA & Canada: 1-800-458-0454
UK, Europe and rest of world call:
+44 (0) 1933 443 863

Young Guardsman
Figure taken from *Warrior 22:*
Imperial Guardsman 1799–1815
Published by Osprey
Illustrated by Christa Hook

Knight, c.1190
Figure taken from *Warrior 1: Norman Knight 950 – 1204AD*
Published by Osprey
Illustrated by Christa Hook

POSTCARD